ONE, TWO, ONE PAIR!

Written and Photo-illustrated by Bruce McMillan

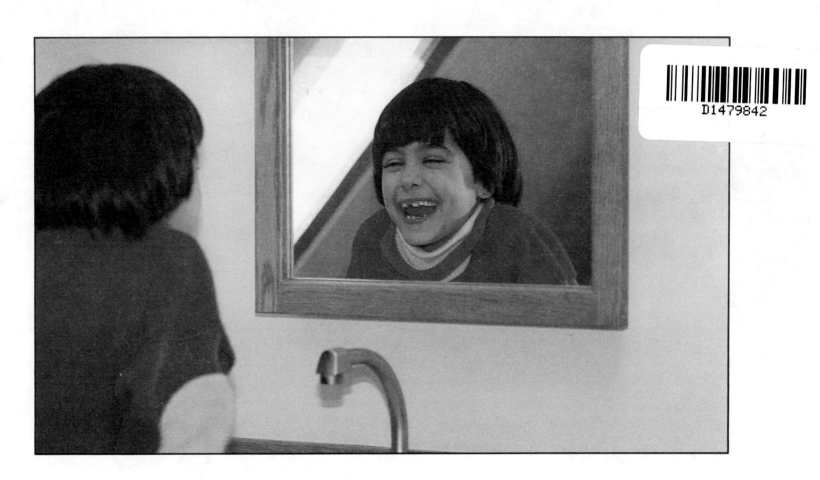

SCHOLASTIC INC.
New York Toronto London Auckland Sydney

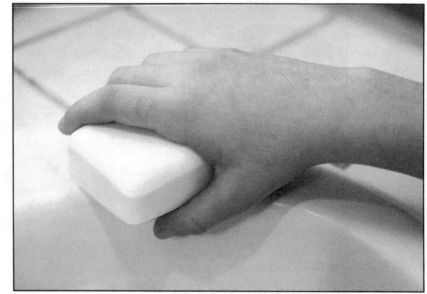

ONE

TWO

ONE PAIR

ONE

TWO

ONE, TWO,
ONE PAIR!

For Elena & Jesse

Design by Bruce McMillan
Art direction by Claire Counihan
Text Set in Optima Medium
Color separations by Color Dot
First edition printed and bound by Horowitz-Rae

ISBN 0-590-43768-2

12 11 10 9 8 7 6 5 4 3 2 1   2 3 4 5 6 7/9

Printed in the U.S.A.   08

ONE PAIR

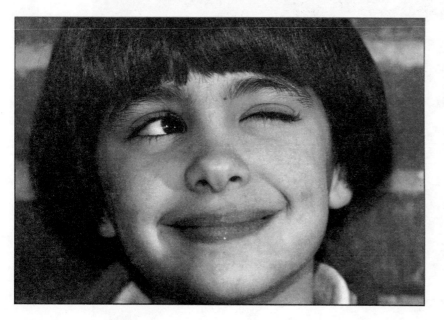

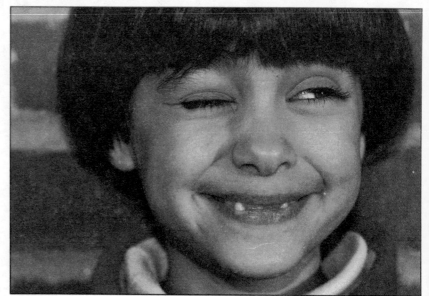

ONE

TWO

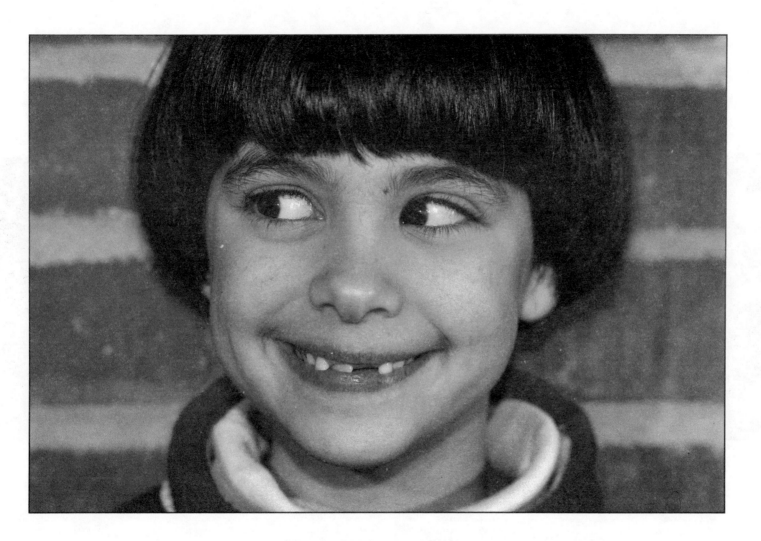

ONE PAIR

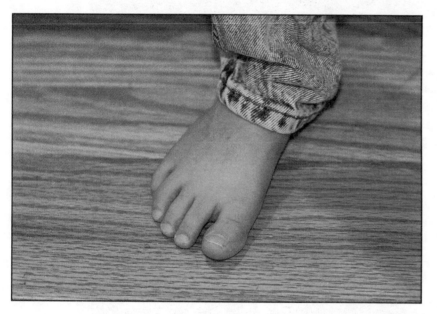

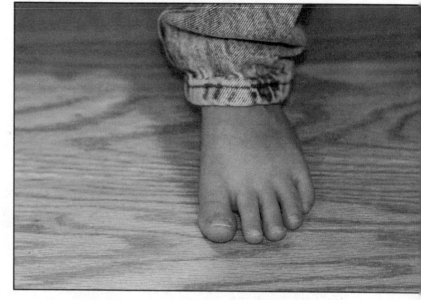

ONE

TWO

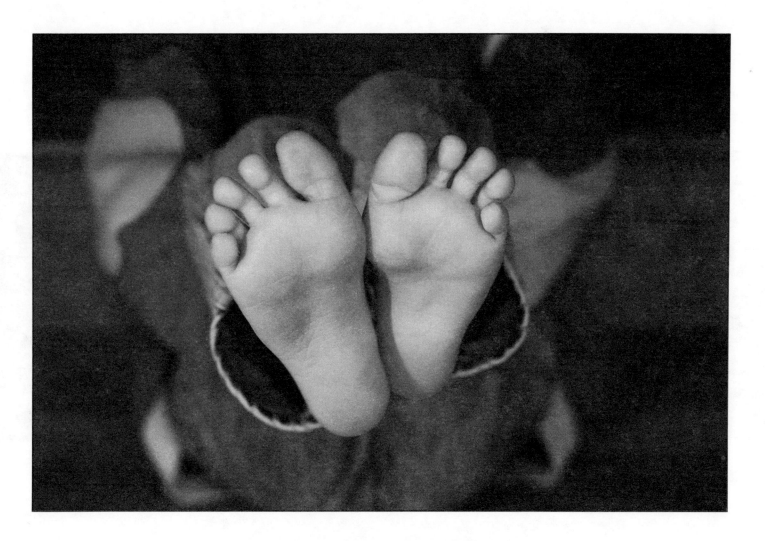

ONE PAIR

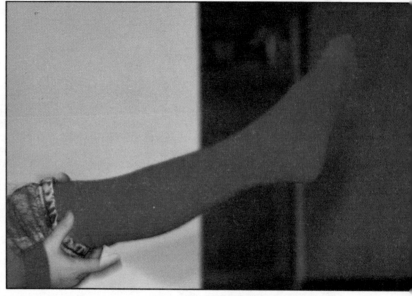

ONE   TWO

ONE PAIR

ONE   TWO

ONE PAIR

ONE

TWO

ONE PAIR

ONE

TWO

ONE PAIR

ONE

TWO

ONE PAIR

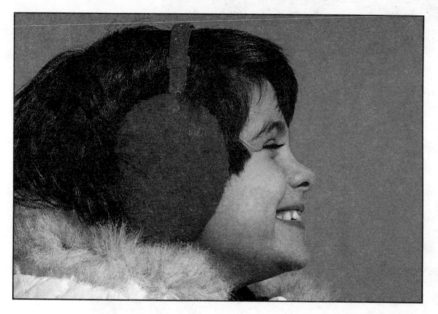

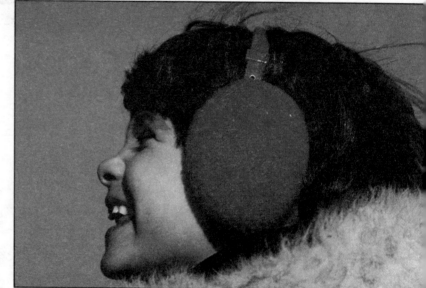

ONE

TWO

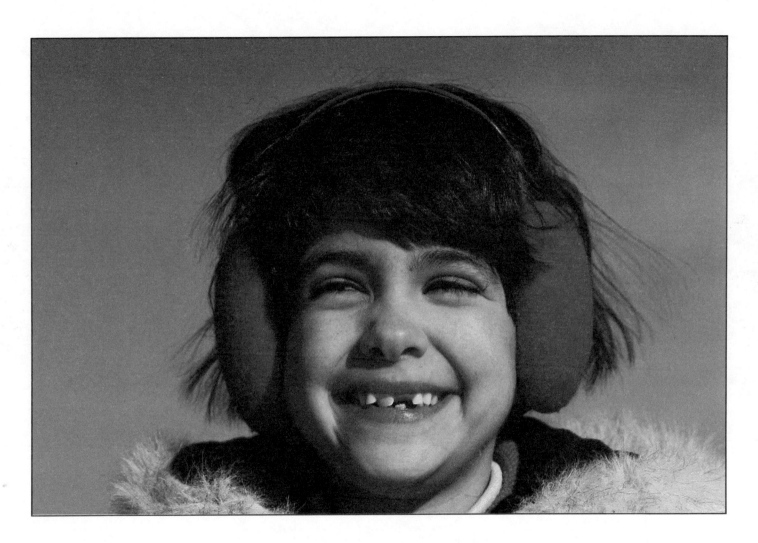

ONE PAIR

ONE

TWO

ONE PAIR

ONE

TWO

ONE PAIR

ONE

TWO

ONE PAIR

ONE

TWO

ONE PAIR

pair (**pair**) *n.* (*pl.* pairs, pair)

1. a set of two corresponding persons or items, similar in form or function and matched or associated.

One, Two, One Pair! is a visual story of getting ready to go ice-skating as well as an introduction to the basic math concept of number sets. This book presents the simplest set of all—the pair. Through the repeating visual pattern (one, two,...one pair) the reader learns to predict logically and to associate what will follow, and so learns to construct a pair. The math skills learned and reinforced—patterns, matching, predicting, and the numerical concept of sets—are all a beginning to mathematical understanding.

Surprise, they're twins! Surprise again! Jessica and Monica Wetherington are not identical twins. They're fraternal twins. It's amusingly confusing trying to tell these two first-graders apart. I met Jessica and Monica when I spoke at their school in Steep Falls, Maine. Finally I'd found twins – a year after developing this book idea. Within days I met with their parents, Brenda and Bruce. To coordinate the book's color scheme, I outfitted Jessica and Monica with new clothes. Over the next six weeks I photographed them on frozen East Sebago Lake, Maine, and at my warm home/studio in Shapleigh, Maine.

One, Two, One Pair! was photo-illustrated using a Nikon FE2 camera with a 55 mm micro or 105 mm Nikkor lens. The exterior lighting was late afternoon or early morning, winter sunlight. The interior lighting was available daylight with two flash units to match the daylight color temperature and a quartz light to warm the colors slightly. The film used was Kodachrome 64, processed by Kodalux.

Coincidentally, the paper that the first edition of this book was printed on was made in Maine at the S. D. Warren paper mill, where Jessica and Monica's grandfather is a papermaker.